CONTENTS

Some words are shown in bold, **like this**. You can find out what they mean by looking in the glossary.

CAN YOU LICK YOUR OWN ELBOW?

Ninety-nine per cent of people try to lick their elbow after reading that question! If you did, too, you probably decided it is impossible.

In fact, a few very **flexible** people *can* manage to get their tongue just about touching their elbow.

long tongue

flexible shoulder

CAN YOUR BRAIN FEEL PAIN?

No! Your brain can tell when *another* part of you is feeling pain. But your brain itself has no pain **sensors** in it. That's why your brain cannot feel any pain.

NOTE: Do NOT try this at home!

Did you know?
Because the brain does not feel pain, people sometimes have **brain surgery** while they're still awake.

WILL I KEEP GROWING FOREVER?

No, you will not keep growing forever. Most people stop growing taller when they are about 16 or 17 years old. Then, after the age of about 40, people start to shrink!

spine shortens

bones may get smaller

By the age of 80, most people are 2.5–7.5 centimetres shorter.

Did you know?
Your ears and your nose *never* stop growing. But after you are born, your eyes hardly grow at all.

DO GIRLS SMELL BETTER THAN BOYS?

When it comes to **sweat**, yes! During and after **puberty**, female sweat is quite a lot less stinky than male sweat. Girls also sweat less than boys.

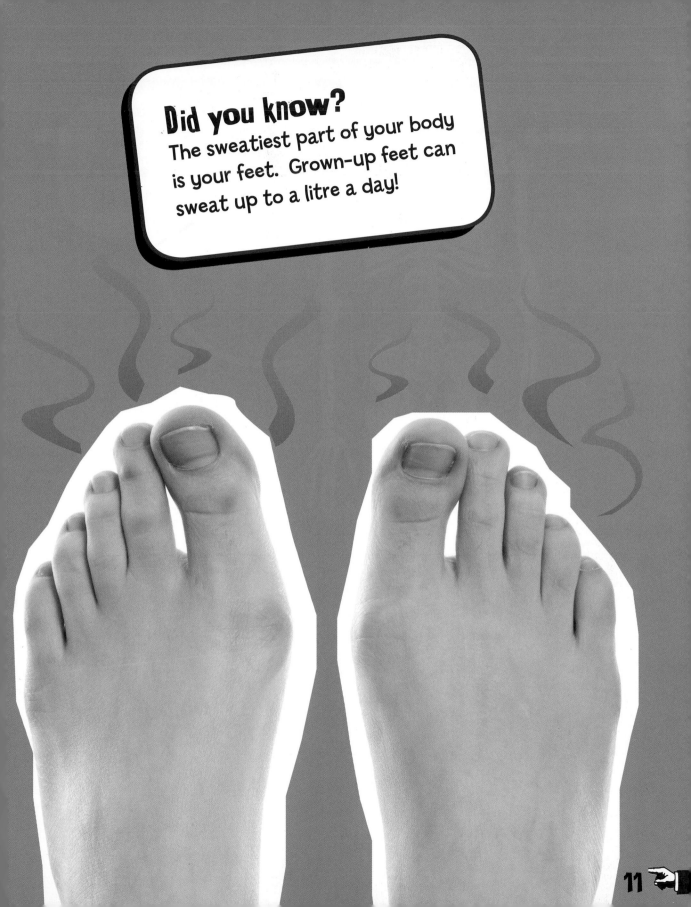

COULD YOU PICK UP A CAR?

You couldn't pick up a whole car and hold it over your head. But humans *have* lifted cars using only their muscles. It usually happens when someone is very scared. Fear causes your body to release a substance called **adrenaline**. This supercharges your muscles.

13

WHICH IS STRONGER – A BABY OR A SHIRE HORSE?

A horse that weighs nearly one tonne is *much* stronger than a 4-kilogram baby, obviously. That's why babies are rubbish at pulling carts and carrying heavy loads!

OK...

However, babies have more strength per kilogram of weight than shire horses. That means a baby weighing almost a tonne would be stronger than a shire horse!

Get out of the way!

15

ARE THERE PEOPLE WHO DON'T FART?

No – everyone farts, even teachers! It's just that some people are better at hiding it than others. Farting is caused by swallowing air, and by **digestion**. The only way not to fart would be not to breathe or eat!

2 + 4 =
3 + 5 =
1 + 2 =

food and air in

digestion

exhaust gas out

Did you know?
People fart an average of 14 times a day.

CAN YOU TICKLE YOURSELF?

No! Feeling ticklish is caused by a fear of being touched by someone else. That's why we wriggle and try to get away. If we try to tickle ourselves, our brain knows not to be scared. That's why we don't react in the same way.

Did you know?

Some animals, including apes and rats, are ticklish, just like humans.

Imagine being asked to find out whether gorillas like being tickled!

IS YOUR SNEEZE FASTER THAN A CHEETAH?

Cheetahs are the fastest land animals. They've been recorded running at 120 kilometres per hour. But some people say that sneezes travel even faster, at 160 kilometres per hour!

In fact, this is not true. Sneezes only travel at about 65 kilometres per hour.

Did you know?
However much you try,
it's impossible to sneeze
with your eyes open.

WHILH CAN YOU GU LONGER WITHOUT — FOOD OR SLEEP?

You feel hungry every few hours, but sleepy only at night-time. So it must be sleep, right? Wrong! A healthy human can last weeks without food. (Do NOT try it, though – it's very bad for you!)

The longest anyone has ever managed without sleep is 11 days. By the end, he was having **hallucinations**!

COULD YOU UPROOT TREES WITH YOUR TONGUE?

No – but it's not such a silly question as it sounds. Your tongue is made of muscles, like an elephant's trunk. And elephants *do* uproot trees with their trunks. With a big enough tongue, maybe you could do the same!

Did you know?
A human tongue once lifted almost 12 kilograms. That's the same as two human babies. Ouch!

WHO HAS MORE BONES — A BABY OR A GROWN-UP?

You might think it would be a great big grown-up – but you'd be wrong! Babies have 50 per cent more bones. As you get older, some of your bones **fuse** together. So you start life with about 300, and end up with just over 200.

full of bones

only two-thirds as many bones as a baby

Did you know?
About a quarter of your bones are in your feet.

WHY DO CROOKS WEAR GLOVES?

Crooks wear gloves so that they don't leave fingerprints behind. There are other prints crooks could leave behind, though. For example, everyone has a **unique** tongue. Imagine catching a criminal using only his tongue print!

Just stick out your tongue please, sir. Aha!

Did you know?

Everyone's ear is slightly different, so ear-prints have been used to identify criminals.

GLOSSARY

adrenaline substance released by the body in frightening or exciting situations. It causes the heart to beat faster and allows the muscles to work better.

brain surgery operation in which the brain itself is cut open

digestion breaking down food into useful parts and waste as it passes through your body

flexible bendy and able to move joints, such as elbows, back, or neck, further than other people

fuse join together

hallucination vision of something that is not actually there, often scary or confusing

puberty time when a child's body starts to become adult or grown-up

sensor something able to detect a physical sensation, such as heat, light, or pain

sweat moisture that comes out through your skin when you are hot. Sweating helps to cool your body down.

unique one of a kind

 30

FIND OUT MORE

Books
The Human Body (100 Facts On), Steve Parker and Belinda Gallagher (Miles Kelly Publishing, 2006)

Body Focus series, Carol Ballard and Steve Parker (Raintree, 2009)

From Armpits to Zits: The Book of Yucky Body Bits, Paul Mason (Wayland, 2011)

Human Beings Can Go Pop in Space! The Fact or Fiction Behind Science (Truth or Busted), Paul Harrison (Wayland, 2012)

Websites
www.gosh.nhs.uk/children/general-health-advice/body-tour
Explore this site to find out facts about the body.

www.kidsbiology.com/human_biology/index.php
Learn about the human body with lots of interactive content on this website.

INDEX

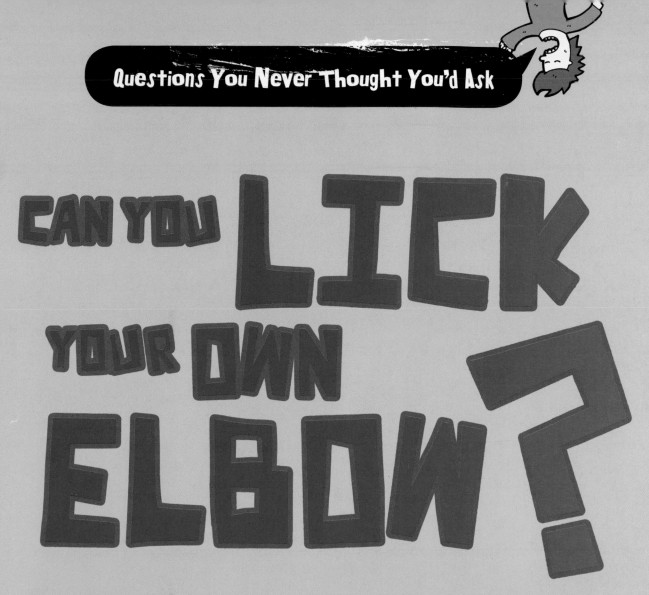

CAN YOU LICK YOUR OWN ELBOW?

And Other Questions About The Human Body

Paul Mason

Raintree is an imprint of Capstone Global Library Limited, a company incorporated in England and Wales having its registered office at 7 Pilgrim Street, London, EC4V 6LB – Registered company number: 6695582

www.raintreepublishers.co.uk
myorders@raintreepublishers.co.uk

Text © Capstone Global Library Limited 2014
First published in hardback in 2014
Paperback edition first published in 2015
The moral rights of the proprietor have been asserted.

Edited by Dan Nunn, Rebecca Rissman, and John-Paul Wilkins
Designed by Steve Mead
Picture research by Mica Brancic
Production by Sophia Argyris
Originated by Capstone Global Library Ltd
Printed and bound in China by CTPS

ISBN 978 1 406 25950 6 (hardback)
17 16 15 14 13
10 9 8 7 6 5 4 3 2 1

ISBN 978 1 406 25956 8 (paperback)
18 17 16 15 14
10 9 8 7 6 5 4 3 2 1

British Library Cataloguing in Publication Data

Mason, Paul.
Can you lick your own elbow? and other questions about the human body. -- (Questions you never thought you'd ask)
612-dc23
A full catalogue record for this book is available from the British Library.

Acknowledgements
We would like to thank the following for permission to reproduce photographs: © Capstone p. 10 boy (Karon Dubke); Getty Images p. 20 man sneezing (Blend Images/John Lund); Photoshot p. 25 (World Illustrated/© De Agostini), Sam dei lune p. 5; Shutterstock pp. 4 (© photobank.ch), 6 brain (© Jeff Banke), 6 hammer (© Ljupco Smokovski), 7 (© VILevi), 8 (© Yuri Arcurs), 9 ears (© Aidar), 9 elderly man (© Valentina R.), 10 girl in field (© Eduard Stelmakh), 11 (© Kacso Sandor), 12 baby (© aporokh at gmail dot com), 12 monster truck (© Gunter Nezhoda), 13 (© mast3r), 14, 15 baby (© Photocrea), 14, 15 horse (© smereka), 16 (© Kacso Sandor), 17 (© Ariwasabi), 18 (© Martin Novak), 19 duster (© Africa Studio), 19 gorilla (© Elliot Hurwitt), 20 cheetah (© photobar), 21 (© Shebeko), 22 criying man (© doglikehorse), 22 bed (© Viktor1), 22 roast duck (© Maksim Toome), 23 top left pig (© Eric Isselée), 23 top right pig, bottom left pig, bottom right pig (© Tsekhmister), 23 wings (© Wallenrock), 23 man (© ARENA Creative), 24 tree (© majeczka), 24 man's tongue (© photobank.ch), 26 (© Africa Studio), 27 (© Reha Mark), 28 man with magnifying glass (© BonD80), 28 man with tongue out (© Dedyukhin Dmitry), 29 (© Cupertino).

Cover photographs of funny man (© photobank.ch) and bicep muscle of thin woman (© Steven Frame) reproduced with permission of Shutterstock.

We would like to thank Diana Bentley and Marla Conn for their invaluable help in the preparation of this book.

Every effort has been made to contact copyright holders of any material reproduced in this book. Any omissions will be rectified in subsequent printings if notice is given to the publisher.